# Marvellous MID-WEEK Meals

*'What's for dinner?' – the question is incessant and the challenge is never ending – to provide food the family will love with the minimum of fuss and maximum of financial finesse.*

*This cookbook is packed with meaty main dishes you can conveniently use to create menus for every occasion. On offer are easy ideas for versatile lean mince and quick sausages. There are one-pot meals to simmer and savour from economy-style meats, as well as old-fashioned family roasts for beef, pork, lamb and chicken. Mid-week meals are a breeze to prepare when you choose from the grills, sautés and stir fries presented here. And, when you've run out of ideas for a special occasion choose from one of the three ready-made menus at the back of the book.*

*These recipes are designed to provide all the flavour and satisfaction you expect, but with today's emphasis on nutrition and healthy eating habits – you'll be proud to serve them to family and friends.*

# CONTENTS

# SAUSAGES AND SAVOURY MINCE

*Main dishes made with sausages, either fresh or smoked, can be as humble as 'bangers and mash' or as gastronomic as Choucroute Garnie. Versatile lean mince – use beef, pork, veal or lamb whichever is the most economic – makes marvellously easy meatballs, loaves, burgers and cottage-style pies that are sure to please both big appetites and little budgets.*

## Pork Sausages with Apples

This is also delicious made using smoked sausages such as kransky (as pictured) or knackwurst.

*750g (1¹/₂lb) thick pork sausages*

*2 large onions, thinly sliced*

*3 large, tart apples, peeled and thinly sliced*

*2 tblspn soft brown sugar*

*1 tblspn wine vinegar*

*2 fresh sage leaves, chopped or pinch dried*

*salt*

*freshly ground black pepper*

**1** Preheat oven to 180°C (350°F/ Gas 4). Pierce sausages several times with a fork and place in a large heavy-based frying pan. Pour over enough cold water to cover and bring to the boil. Reduce heat and simmer for 5 minutes.

**2** Pour off water and cook sausages over low heat until brown on all sides. Pierce sausages once and place in a single layer in a shallow ovenproof dish.

**3** Cook onions in fat remaining in pan over moderate heat, stirring, for 3 minutes or until soft. Add apples, sugar, vinegar and sage and cook for 2-3 minutes longer or until apples begin to soften. Season to taste.

**4** Spoon onion mixture over sausages and bake for 20 minutes or until sausages are cooked and apples are tender.

*Serves 6*

## Sausages with Onion Gravy

For a complete meal serve with creamy mashed potatoes and steamed cabbage.

*8 pork sausages*

*60g (2oz) butter*

*6 onions, sliced*

*2 tblspn plain flour*

*1 tspn dry mustard*

*250ml (8fl oz) beef stock*

*185ml (6fl oz) flat beer*

*1 tspn sugar*

*1 tspn chopped fresh thyme or pinch dried*

*1 tspn chopped fresh sage or pinch dried*

*salt*

*freshly ground black pepper*

**1** Pierce sausages and place in a saucepan of cold water. Bring to the boil and simmer for 10 minutes. Drain and remove skins.

**2** Melt butter in a saucepan and cook onions over moderate heat, stirring, for 3-5 minutes or until soft. Stir in flour and mustard and cook for 1 minute. Off the heat, gradually stir in stock and beer. Add sugar and herbs and season to taste. Bring to the boil, then simmer, stirring, for 15 minutes. Add sausages and simmer for 5 minutes or until heated through.

*Serves 4*

*Clockwise from top: Pork Sausages with Apples, Sausages with Onion Gravy, Frankfurters served with potato salad*

# Frankfurters with Creole Sauce

6-8 Continental frankfurters or other large, meaty frankfurters of your choice.

### Creole Sauce

30g (1oz) butter

1 small onion, finely chopped

1 clove garlic, crushed

1 small green pepper, finely chopped

2 stalks celery, chopped

440g (14oz) can tomatoes, undrained and mashed

2 tspn soft brown sugar

salt

Tabasco sauce

**1** Preheat oven to 200°C (400°F/ Gas 6). Arrange frankfurters in a single layer in an ovenproof dish.

**2** To make sauce, melt butter in a saucepan and cook onion, garlic, green pepper and celery over moderate heat, stirring, for 10 minutes or until soft. Add tomatoes, sugar, salt and Tabasco sauce to taste and bring to the boil. Lower heat and simmer for 5 minutes.

**3** Spoon sauce over frankfurters. Bake for 15 minutes or until frankfurters are cooked and sauce thickens.

*Serves 4*

# Frikadeller

Danish meat patties are traditionally accompanied by red cabbage, boiled or mashed potatoes, beetroot and a cucumber salad. They are equally good made just with pork mince.

750g (1 1/2lb) pork and veal mince or 375g (12oz) each lean pork mince and lean veal mince

45g (1 1/2oz) breadcrumbs, made from stale bread

90ml (3fl oz) milk

1 onion, grated

1 egg

1 tspn ground nutmeg

1/2 tspn salt

1/2 tspn freshly ground white pepper

seasoned flour

30g (1oz) butter

2 tblspn vegetable oil

sour cream and pickles, to serve

**1** Place meat in a large bowl. Soak breadcrumbs in milk, then beat, a little at a time, into meat. Add onion, egg, nutmeg, salt and white pepper and beat until light and fluffy. Cover and chill for 1 hour or until mixture is firm.

**2** Shape mixture into small, thick patties and dust with seasoned flour. Heat butter and oil in a large, heavy-based frying pan over moderate heat and cook patties for 8-10 minutes each side or until cooked to your liking. Serve with sour cream and pickles.

*Serves 4*

# Porcupines

As the rice cooks the grains stand out, resembling porcupine quills.

500g (1lb) lean beef mince

30g (1oz) breadcrumbs, made from stale bread

3/4 tspn salt

1/2 tspn paprika

1 egg, beaten

100g (3 1/2oz) uncooked rice

315g (10oz) can condensed tomato soup

125ml (4fl oz) water

125g (4oz) frozen peas

**1** Place beef, breadcrumbs, salt, paprika and egg in a bowl and mix well to combine. Shape mixture into balls, flatten slightly, then roll in rice to coat.

**2** Heat soup and water in a large, heavy-based frying pan over moderate heat, stirring, until simmering. Add patties, reduce heat, cover and simmer gently for 40 minutes. Stir in peas and simmer for 5 minutes longer or until patties and peas are cooked.

*Serves 4*

# Shepherd's Pie

1 tblspn vegetable oil

500g (1lb) lean beef mince or finely chopped leftover roast meat

1 large onion, chopped

salt

freshly ground black pepper

1 tblspn Worcestershire sauce

250ml (8fl oz) tomato juice or leftover gravy

2 firm-ripe tomatoes, peeled and sliced

### Potato Topping

750g (1 1/2lb) old potatoes, peeled and cubed

2 tblspn hot milk

15g (1/2oz) butter

1 egg, beaten

1 tblspn freshly grated Parmesan cheese

**1** Heat oil in a large, heavy-based frying pan and cook beef over moderate heat, stirring to break up any lumps, until brown. Add onion and cook, stirring, until onion is soft. (If using cooked meat, fry onion first, then stir in meat and brown it).

**2** Season to taste with salt and black pepper, add Worcestershire sauce and tomato juice or gravy, cover and simmer gently for 30 minutes. Spoon mixture into a 1.5 litre (2 1/2pt) ovenproof dish and top with tomatoes.

**3** To make topping, cook potatoes in boiling salted water until tender. Drain well and mash with milk, butter, egg and season to taste. Spoon over tomatoes, rough the surface with a fork and sprinkle with Parmesan cheese.

**4** Preheat oven to 180°C (350°F/ Gas 4). Bake pie for 30 minutes or until hot. Place under a preheated moderate grill and cook for 2-3 minutes or until topping is brown and crisp.

*Serves 6*

*Frikadellar*

*Meatballs with Lemon and Caper Sauce*

## Meatballs with Lemon and Caper Sauce

If veal mince is unavailable make these meatballs using just pork mince.

2 slices white bread, roughly crumbled

2 tblspn double cream

15g (1/2oz) butter

2 onions, finely chopped

375g (12oz) pork and veal mince or 185g (6oz) each lean pork mince and lean veal mince

185g (6oz) lean beef mince

2-3 canned anchovy fillets, rinsed and finely chopped

2 tblspn finely chopped fresh parsley

1/2 tspn finely grated lemon rind

2 eggs

salt

freshly ground black pepper

### Court Bouillon

1.5 litres (2 1/2pt) water

1 small onion, peeled and studded with 1 whole clove

1 small bay leaf

### Lemon Caper Sauce

60g (2oz) butter

30g (1oz) plain flour

3 tblspn strained, freshly squeezed lemon juice

1 tblspn drained capers

2 egg yolks, lightly beaten

2 tblspn chopped fresh parsley

2 tblspn sour cream

**1** Soak bread in cream in a large bowl until cream is absorbed. Melt butter in a small saucepan and cook onions over low heat, stirring, until soft. Allow to cool.

**2** Stir onions into bread, add meat, anchovies, parsley, lemon rind, eggs and salt and black pepper to taste and mix to combine. Shape into twelve balls.

**3** To make bouillon, place water, onion, bay leaf and 1 teaspoon salt in a saucepan and bring to the boil. Simmer for 10 minutes. Add meatballs and simmer for 15 minutes or until meatballs float and are cooked. Place meatballs in a serving dish and keep warm. Reserve cooking liquid.

**4** To make sauce, melt butter in a saucepan, stir in flour and cook over moderate heat for 1 minute. Remove pan from heat and gradually blend in 750ml (1 1/4pt) reserved liquid. Cook, stirring constantly, until sauce boils and thickens. Add lemon juice and capers and simmer gently for 5 minutes.

**5** Stir a little hot sauce into egg yolks, return mixture to pan and cook, without boiling and stirring constantly, until sauce thickens slightly. Add parsley and sour cream and season to taste. Pour sauce over meatballs and serve.

*Serves 6*

## Choucroute Garnie

This wonderfully flavoured main dish makes a great winter meal when served with rye bread, boiled potatoes and German-style mustard.

1kg (2lb) sauerkraut, preferably from vacuum packed bags or refrigerated jars

125g (4oz) lean bacon, roughly diced

1 tblspn vegetable oil

1 large onion, chopped

3 carrots, diced

1 unpeeled Granny Smith apple, diced or grated

1 tspn caraway seeds

1 bouquet garni (parsley, thyme, bay leaf)

8 juniper berries

250ml (8fl oz) dry white wine

1 litre (1³/4pt) chicken stock

45g (1¹/2oz) butter

500g (1lb) lean diced pork

500g (1lb) smoked pork sausage such as kransky or knackwurst, cut into thick diagonal slices

3-4 tblspn chopped fresh parsley

**1** Soak sauerkraut in cold water for 30 minutes. Drain. Cook bacon in a frying pan over moderate heat for 5 minutes. Add oil, onion and carrots and cook, stirring, for 8 minutes or until onion is golden.

**2** Place sauerkraut in a flameproof casserole, stir in bacon mixture, apple and caraway seeds. Add bouquet garni, juniper berries, wine and enough stock to just cover mixture. Top with buttered greaseproof paper and bring to simmering. Cover with lid and simmer for 2 hours, adding stock as needed to prevent the mixture from drying out.

**3** Melt butter in a frying pan and cook pork over moderate heat, stirring, until golden. Add pork and sausage to casserole, cover and simmer for 2 hours or until pork is tender. Remove bouquet garni and sprinkle with parsley.

*Serves 6*

## Meatloaf with Spicy Sauce

1 egg, beaten

125ml (4fl oz) evaporated milk

1 tblspn vinegar

1 tblspn treacle

1 tblspn French mustard

90g (3oz) breadcrumbs, made from stale bread

1 small onion, finely chopped

¹/2 tspn salt

750g (1¹/2lb) lean beef mince

**Spicy Sauce**

2 tblspn cornflour

2 tspn dry mustard

125ml (4fl oz) cold water

2 tspn vinegar

1 tspn treacle

250ml (8fl oz) beef stock

**1** Preheat oven to 180°C (350°F/ Gas 4). Combine egg, evaporated milk, vinegar, treacle, mustard, breadcrumbs, onion and salt in a bowl. Add beef and mix to combine. Pack mixture into a 14 x 21cm (5¹/2 x 8¹/2in) loaf tin and bake for 1¹/4 hours or until cooked.

**2** To make sauce, combine cornflour and mustard in a saucepan and slowly stir in water. Add vinegar, treacle and stock and cook over moderate heat, stirring constantly, until sauce boils and thickens. Serve with meatloaf.

*Serves 6*

*Choucroute Garnie*

## Beef Terrine with Ham

500g (1lb) boneless lean beef

250g (8oz) thickly sliced cooked ham

250g (8oz) bacon, in one piece

1 tspn ground allspice

4 tblspn chopped fresh parsley

2 tblspn chopped mixed fresh herbs such as chervil, thyme and tarragon

1 small bay leaf, crumbled

2 cloves garlic, chopped

3 tblspn brandy

salt

freshly ground black pepper

2 tblspn water or stock

1 tblspn gelatine

**1** Preheat oven to 180°C (350°F/ Gas 4). Cut beef, ham and bacon into very thin strips. Toss beef strips with allspice, parsley, mixed herbs, bay leaf, garlic, brandy and salt and black pepper to taste.

**2** Layer beef, ham and bacon in a terrine dish or loaf tin, beginning with the bacon and ending with the beef. Add water or stock and cover tightly with lid or foil. Place terrine or tin in a baking dish and pour in enough hot water to come halfway up the sides of the terrine or tin. Bake for 1½ hours or until cooked.

**3** Pour cooking juices from terrine into a heatproof bowl. Sprinkle gelatine over juices and stir over simmering water until gelatine dissolves. Pour mixture back into terrine.

**4** Cover terrine with aluminium foil, place a light weight on top and cool. Remove weight, cover and refrigerate for 2-3 days. Serve from the mould cut into slices.

*Serves 8*

## Mexican Beef Casserole

Mexican chilli powder is a mixture of chilli powder, cumin, oregano, black pepper and garlic and has a mild flavour. If you want a hotter dish, add Tabasco sauce to taste.

1 tblspn vegetable oil

500g (1lb) lean beef mince

1 large onion, chopped

3 stalks celery, sliced

½ green or red pepper, diced

220g (7oz) uncooked long-grain rice

440g (14oz) can tomatoes, undrained and mashed

250ml (8fl oz) water

½ tspn Worcestershire sauce

1-2 tspn Mexican chilli powder

75g (2½oz) halved and pitted black olives, optional

salt

freshly ground black pepper

**1** Preheat oven to 160°C (325°F/ Gas 3). Heat oil in a flameproof casserole and cook beef over moderate heat, stirring, until brown. Push beef to one side, add onion, celery and green or red pepper and cook, stirring, until onion is brown.

**2** Add rice, tomatoes, water, Worcestershire sauce, chilli powder, olives (if using) and salt and black pepper to taste. Mix well, cover and bake for 45-60 minutes or until rice is tender.

*Serves 6*

## Neapolitan Patties

750g (1½lb) lean beef mince

1 onion, finely chopped

2 cloves garlic, crushed

60g (2oz) breadcrumbs, made from stale bread

60g (2oz) pine nuts

30g (1oz) freshly grated Parmesan cheese

4-6 tblspn finely chopped fresh parsley

1½ tspn salt

1 tspn freshly ground black pepper

1 tspn dried oregano leaves

2 eggs, beaten

Combine all ingredients in a bowl. Shape mixture into six thick patties and cook under a preheated hot grill for 5 minutes each side or until brown and crispy.

*Serves 6*

## Fresh Herb Terrine

500g (1lb) lean pork mince

125g (4oz) pork or calves liver, minced

90g (3oz) streaky bacon rashers, minced

375g (12oz) young spinach or silverbeet, stems removed

2-3 leaves fresh sorrel or ½ tspn finely grated lemon rind

1 onion, finely chopped

1 large clove garlic, finely chopped

1 large egg, beaten

90g (3oz) ham, diced

1 tblspn chopped fresh parsley

1 tblspn chopped fresh basil leaves

2-3 leaves fresh thyme or pinch dried

salt

freshly ground black pepper

ground nutmeg

60g (2oz) plain flour blended with 2 tblspn water

**1** Preheat oven to 160°C (325°F/ Gas 3). Combine pork, liver and bacon in a bowl. Blanch spinach or silverbeet and sorrel (if using) in boiling water, drain well and chop finely. Add to meat mixture with onion, garlic, egg, ham, herbs and salt, black pepper and nutmeg to taste. Mix to combine.

**2** Pack mixture into an oiled terrine dish, cover with a double thickness of aluminium foil, then terrine lid and seal using the flour and water paste. Bake for 1¼ hours. Remove lid and bake for 15 minutes longer or until brown.

**3** Remove from oven, place a weight over the foil, cool then refrigerate overnight. Serve terrine cut into thin slices with wholemeal bread and pickles.

*Serves 8*

**Kitchen Tip**

If you do not have a terrine dish this terrine can be cooked in a loaf tin covered with four thickness of aluminium foil.

*Fresh Herb Terrine, Beef Terrine with Ham*

## Aberdeen Sausage

500g (1lb) lean beef mince

250g (8oz) bacon, minced

60g (2oz) breadcrumbs, made from stale bread

1 egg, beaten

1 tblspn finely chopped fresh parsley

1 tspn salt

1/2 tspn ground nutmeg

1 tspn finely grated lemon rind

2 tspn Worcestershire sauce

freshly ground black pepper

plain flour for dusting

dried breadcrumbs for coating

**1** Place beef, bacon, breadcrumbs, egg, parsley, salt, nutmeg, lemon rind, Worcestershire sauce and black pepper to taste in a bowl and mix well to combine. Shape mixture into a log about 8cm (3in) thick and dust evenly with flour.

**2** Tie log securely in a scalded, floured pudding cloth, or wrap in foil sealing edges well, and carefully lower into a saucepan of boiling water. Boil for 2 hours, adding more hot water as needed. Drain and unwrap.

**3** Preheat oven to 150°C (300°F/ Gas 2). Roll hot log in dried breadcrumbs to coat, place on a lightly greased baking sheet and bake for 15 minutes or until log is dry. Cool, then refrigerate until firm. Serve cut into slices.

*Serves 6*

## Indian Lentil Burgers

Green masala paste is available from Asian food shops and some supermarkets. It keeps for months in the refrigerator.

100g (3 1/2oz) red lentils or 125g (4oz) split peas

1 tblspn chopped onion

salt

500g (1lb) lean beef mince

1 egg

2 tspn green masala paste

ghee or vegetable oil for frying

**1** Soak lentils or peas in cold water for 1 hour, drain and place in a saucepan. Add onion and 250ml (8fl oz) water and bring to the boil. Lower heat and simmer gently, uncovered, until lentils are soft and water is absorbed. Mash lentils and season with salt. Cool.

**2** Combine beef, egg, masala paste and lentil mixture. Shape mixture into eight patties. Heat a little ghee or oil in a frying pan and cook patties over moderate heat for 5 minutes each side or until cooked to your liking.

*Serves 4*

## Meatballs Avgolemono

500g (1lb) lean beef mince

1 small onion, chopped

2 tblspn uncooked rice

1 tblspn chopped fresh parsley

2 tspn chopped fresh mint

salt

freshly ground black pepper

375ml (12fl oz) beef stock

250ml (8fl oz) water

2 tspn cornflour blended with 2 tblspn cold water

2 eggs

2-3 tblspn freshly squeezed lemon juice

**1** Place beef, onion, rice, parsley, mint and salt and black pepper to taste in a bowl and mix to combine. Stir in 60ml (2fl oz) stock, then shape mixture into small balls.

**2** Bring remaining stock and water to the boil in a large saucepan. Add meatballs, lower heat and simmer for 10 minutes or until cooked. Stir in cornflour mixture and simmer, stirring constantly, until sauce thickens.

**3** Beat eggs with lemon juice until thick. Gradually stir 250ml (8fl oz) hot sauce into egg mixture, then return mixture to saucepan and mix well. Remove pan from heat, cover and stand for 5 minutes before serving.

*Serves 4*

## Cassoulet with Garlic Butter

500g (1lb) dried haricot beans

125g (4oz) fresh pork rind, cut into small squares

750g (1 1/2lb) pickled pork, in one piece

500g (1lb) bratwurst, or smoked sausages such as kransky or knackwurst

freshly ground black pepper

**Garlic Butter**

8 cloves garlic

90g (3oz) butter

3-4 tblspn finely chopped fresh parsley

**1** Soak beans in cold water overnight. Drain, place in a saucepan, cover with fresh water, bring to the boil and boil for 15 minutes. Remove pan from heat and stand for 1 hour. Drain.

**2** Preheat oven to 160°C (325°F/ Gas 3). Place pork rind in a large, deep casserole and top with pickled pork and drained beans. Add enough boiling water to just cover beans. Cover tightly and bake for 3 hours.

**3** Cook bratwurst or smoked sausages under a preheated moderate grill for 5 minutes or until brown. If using smoked sausages, cut them into thick slices. Add sausages to casserole and mix to combine. Season to taste with black pepper and bake, uncovered, for 20 minutes.

**4** To make Garlic Butter, simmer garlic in lightly salted water for 10 minutes, drain and pound to a paste with butter. Stir in parsley.

**5** Remove casserole from oven, remove pork and sausages and cut pork into thick slices. Stir butter mixture into bean mixture. To serve, spoon bean mixture onto a large platter, then top with sausages and pork.

*Serves 6*

# CLASSIC AND CLEVER NEW CASSEROLES

*A large, heavy-based, flameproof casserole with a tight-fitting lid is indispensable for braising. With it, you can cook over heat and bake in the same dish, omitting the need to sauté or brown foods first in a frying pan. If you don't have such a treasure, use a large, heavy-based saucepan instead and simmer these recipes on the back of the cooker top or brown first in a frying pan then transfer to a casserole and bake in the oven.*

## Navarin of Lamb

When available use baby turnips and beetroot and young green beans and leave them whole.

1 tblspn olive oil

1kg (2lb) boneless shoulder lamb, cut into 5cm (2in) cubes

1 tblspn plain flour

1 tspn sugar

4 firm-ripe tomatoes, peeled and quartered or 440g (14oz) can tomatoes, undrained and mashed

500ml (16fl oz) beef stock

2 cloves garlic, bruised

1 sprig fresh rosemary leaves or 1 tspn dried

1 bouquet garni

salt

freshly ground black pepper

2 bunches mature spring onions, trimmed, with some green tops left on

3-4 white turnips, peeled and quartered or 12 baby turnips

3-4 beetroot, quartered or 12 baby beetroot

250g (8oz) green beans, trimmed

30g (1oz) butter

**1** Heat oil in a flameproof casserole and cook lamb, in batches, over moderate heat until brown. Return lamb to casserole, stir in flour and sugar and cook for 3 minutes.

**2** Add tomatoes, stock, garlic, rosemary, bouquet garni and salt and black pepper to taste and bring to the boil. Lower heat and simmer gently, partially covered, for 1 1/2 hours, adding a little extra stock if needed to prevent drying out.

**3** Boil or microwave vegetables, separately, until just tender. Slip skins off beetroot when slightly cooled.

**4** Just prior to serving, melt butter in a large, heavy-based frying pan and cook vegetables, stirring, over moderate heat until hot.

**5** Remove bouquet garni from lamb mixture and discard. Transfer lamb to a serving dish, reserving some gravy. Scatter vegetables over lamb, spoon over reserved gravy and serve.

*Serves 6*

*Navarin of Lamb*

## Spiced Beef Pot Roast

1.5kg (3lb) boneless piece of beef suitable for pot roasting

2 tblspn vegetable oil

1 large onion, sliced

1 clove garlic, crushed

2 tblspn tomato purée

60ml (2fl oz) red wine

125ml (4fl oz) water

1 small onion, studded with 3 whole cloves

3 thin strips orange rind

1 tspn brown sugar

1/2 tspn ground nutmeg

1/2 tspn ground cinnamon

salt

freshly ground black pepper

**1** Tie meat into a neat shape. Heat oil in a flameproof casserole and cook meat over moderate heat until brown on all sides. Remove and set aside.

**2** Add sliced onion and garlic to casserole and cook over moderate heat, stirring, until onion is soft. Add tomato purée, wine, water, whole onion, orange rind, sugar, spices and salt and black pepper to taste, stir well and return meat to casserole.

**3** Bring to the boil, then lower heat, cover and simmer gently, turning meat occasionally, for 2-2 1/2 hours or until meat is tender. Transfer meat to a serving plate and keep warm.

**4** Discard whole onion and orange rind, bring liquid to the boil and boil for 10 minutes or until liquid reduces and thickens. Slice meat and accompany with sauce.

*Serves 6*

### Kitchen Tip
Leftover pot roasts reheat well in their own sauces. Store meat and sauce separately in the refrigerator for up to 4 days. Heat sauce to boiling, add sliced meat and simmer gently until heated. For longer storage, place sliced meat in a freezerproof container, cover with sauce, seal, label and freeze for up to 2 months.

To serve, thaw in refrigerator overnight, transfer to a saucepan and simmer gently, covered, until heated through.

## Pot-au-Feu

Any leftover stock can be simmered with a few fresh peas and egg noodles to make a delicious soup.

1.5-2kg (3-4lb) boneless piece of beef suitable for pot roasting

2-3 shin bones

2 onions, unpeeled and quartered

3 carrots, sliced

2 parsnips, sliced

2 leeks, trimmed and halved lengthwise

2 stalks celery, chopped

1 large clove garlic, bruised

1 bouquet garni

2 whole cloves

6 black peppercorns

1 tblspn salt

1 x 1.5kg (3lb) chicken, optional

### Glazed Vegetables

assorted vegetables of your choice such as baby carrots, tiny new potatoes, parsnips, Brussels sprouts

1-2 tblspn sugar

**1** Place beef and bones in a large deep saucepan and pour over enough cold water to just cover. Bring very slowly to the boil — this can take up to an hour — using a slotted spoon skim off any scum as it foams. Add 250ml (8fl oz) cold water and skim again, this is important for a good clear stock.

**2** Add onions, carrots, parsnips, leeks, celery, garlic, bouquet garni, cloves, black peppercorns and salt and bring to simmering. Simmer gently, partially covered, for 2 hours. Add chicken (if using) and simmer for 1 hour longer or until beef and chicken are tender.

**3** Transfer beef and chicken to a serving platter. Keep warm. Strain stock through muslin or a double thickness of paper towel into a bowl, pressing vegetables to extract as much liquid as possible. Discard vegetables and return stock to a clean saucepan.

**4** To glaze vegetables, cook chosen vegetables, separately, in a little simmering stock until just tender. Place sugar and 125ml (4fl oz) stock in a frying pan and bring to the boil, stirring until sugar dissolves. Boil until liquid reduces and thickens, add vegetables and heat, stirring, until vegetables are glazed. Serve with beef and chicken.

*Serves 6-8*

## Braised Pork Italian-style

This is a good recipe for rindless joints of pork, otherwise, ask the butcher to remove the rind for you.

1.25kg (2 1/2lb) leg of pork, rind removed

salt

freshly ground black pepper

1 clove garlic, cut into slivers

1 tblspn butter

2 onions, finely chopped

2 carrots, sliced

1 litre (1 3/4pt) boiling milk

1 bay leaf

1 sprig fresh rosemary leaves or 1/2 tspn dried

1 tspn plain flour blended with 1 tblspn butter, optional

**1** Rub pork all over with salt and black pepper. Make small slits in surface of pork and insert garlic slivers. Melt butter in a flameproof casserole and cook pork over moderate heat until brown on all sides. Add onions and carrots and cook, stirring, until golden.

**2** Add enough hot milk to cover pork by 1.5cm (5/8in), add bay leaf and rosemary, lower heat and simmer very gently, uncovered, for 1 hour. Turn meat over and cook for 1 hour longer, or until meat is tender and sauce reduces to 250ml (8fl oz).

**3** If sauce is too thin, stir in flour mixture and cook, stirring constantly without boiling, for 5 minutes or until sauce thickens. Slice pork and serve with sauce.

*Serves 6*

*Pot-au-Feu*

*Veal Stew Provençal*

## Veal Stew Provençal

This stew can also be made using lamb instead of veal.

60ml (2fl oz) olive oil

3 onions, chopped

3 large cloves garlic, crushed

1kg (2lb) boneless lean veal, cut into 3cm (1¼in) pieces

4 thin strips orange rind

440g (14oz) can tomatoes, undrained and mashed or 4 large firm-ripe tomatoes, peeled, seeded and quartered

250ml (8fl oz) dry white wine

1 sprig fresh thyme or ¼ tspn dried

1 sprig fresh rosemary leaves or ¼ tspn dried

250g (8oz) pickling onions or small white onions, peeled

250g (8oz) carrots, cut into thick matchsticks

salt

freshly ground black pepper

75g (2½oz) black olives

**1** Heat oil in a large flameproof casserole and cook chopped onions and 2 cloves garlic over moderate heat, stirring, until onions are soft. Add veal, orange rind, tomatoes, wine and herbs and bring to the boil. Lower heat and simmer gently for 45 minutes or until veal is tender.

**2** Add pickling onions and carrots and simmer for 15 minutes or until vegetables are tender. Season to taste with salt and black pepper. Just prior to serving, add olives and remaining garlic and heat gently for 5 minutes longer or until heated through.

*Serves 4*

## Rabbit with Tarragon

Delicious served with French bread and a green crisp salad.

2 x 1kg (2lb) rabbits, cut into pieces

125ml (4fl oz) olive oil

30g (1oz) butter

2 onions, sliced

3 stalks celery, cut into matchsticks

2 large carrots, cut into matchsticks

1 bulb fresh fennel, cut into 8 slices

125ml (4fl oz) dry white wine

6-8 sprigs fresh parsley

6 cloves garlic, peeled

1 bay leaf

2 tspn dried tarragon

1 tspn salt

freshly ground black pepper

**1** Preheat oven to 190°C (375°F/ Gas 5). Brush rabbit with some of the oil. Heat remaining oil and butter in a flameproof casserole and cook rabbit over moderate heat until golden. Set aside.

**2** Add onions, celery, carrots and fennel to casserole and sauté until golden. Return rabbit to casserole, add wine, parsley, garlic, bay leaf, tarragon and salt and black pepper to taste.

**3** Cover tightly and bake for 1½ hours or until rabbit is tender. Discard parsley.

*Serves 6-8*

# Burgundy Beef

750g (1¹/₂lb) lean stewing steak, cut into 2.5cm (1in) cubes

2 carrots, thinly sliced

6 black peppercorns

3 sprigs fresh parsley

¹/₄ tspn dried thyme leaves

1 bay leaf

315ml (10fl oz) red wine

2 tblspn olive oil

30g (1oz) butter

2 onions, thinly sliced

16 pickling onions or small white onions, peeled

2 rashers streaky bacon, cut into strips

2 tblspn brandy

2 tblspn plain flour

1 clove garlic, crushed

170ml (5¹/₂fl oz) beef stock

salt

freshly ground black pepper

1 bouquet garni

125g (4oz) button mushrooms

2 tblspn finely chopped fresh parsley

**1** Place steak, carrots, black peppercorns, herbs and half the wine in a bowl, cover and marinate in the refrigerator overnight. Drain, reserving marinade. Pat meat dry.

**2** Heat oil and butter in a large, flameproof casserole and cook sliced onions, whole onions and bacon over moderate heat until golden. Using a slotted spoon, remove mixture and set aside.

**3** Cook steak, in batches, in casserole until brown on all sides. Return steak to pan. Heat brandy, ignite and pour over meat. When flames subside, sprinkle meat with flour, add garlic, stock, reserved marinade and remaining wine and bring to simmering, stirring constantly.

**4** Return onion mixture to casserole. Season to taste with salt and black pepper, add bouquet garni and mushrooms and simmer gently, partially covered, for 1-1¹/₄ hours or until beef is tender.

**5** Transfer meat, whole onions and mushrooms to a serving dish and keep warm. Discard bay leaf and bouquet garni and simmer sauce until thickened. Strain sauce and pour over meat. Sprinkle with parsley and serve.

*Serves 6*

# Italian Lamb Casserole

2 tblspn olive oil

2 rashers bacon, diced

1 onion, sliced

2 cloves garlic, crushed

1.5kg (3lb) lean boneless lamb, cut into 3cm (1¹/₄in) cubes

125ml (4fl oz) red wine, plus 2 tblspn

2 tspn chopped fresh oregano

salt and freshly ground black pepper

2 tblspn tomato purée

2 firm-ripe tomatoes, peeled, seeded and quartered

8-10 pitted black olives

**1** Heat oil in a large flameproof casserole and cook bacon, onion and garlic over moderate heat until golden. Using a slotted spoon remove mixture and set aside.

**2** Cook lamb, in batches, in casserole until brown on all sides. Add 125ml (4fl oz) wine, oregano and salt and black pepper to taste and bring to simmering.

**3** Simmer for 10-15 minutes or until liquid reduces by half. Add bacon mixture, tomato purée, tomatoes and olives, cover and simmer gently for 1¹/₄ hours, or until lamb is tender. Stir in remaining 2 tablespoons wine.

*Serves 6-8*

*Burgundy Beef*

## Braised Rolled Shoulder of Lamb

60g (2oz) breadcrumbs, made from stale bread

6-8 mushrooms, chopped

4-6 tblspn chopped fresh parsley

1 sprig fresh thyme, leaves removed, or 1/2 tspn dried

1 clove garlic, chopped

salt

freshly ground black pepper

1.5kg (3lb) shoulder of lamb, boned and rolled

2 onions, sliced

1kg (2lb) baby new potatoes

125ml (4fl oz) white wine or water

chopped fresh parsley, to serve

**1** Preheat oven to 190°C (375°F/ Gas 5). Combine breadcrumbs, mushrooms, parsley, thyme, garlic and salt and black pepper to taste. Unroll lamb, spread with stuffing, reroll and tie into a neat shape.

**2** Place lamb in an oiled casserole dish, scatter with onions and surround with potatoes. Add wine or water and sprinkle with salt and black pepper to taste. Cover and bake for 1¹/₂ hours or until lamb is tender.

**3** Remove string from lamb, slice and arrange on a serving platter with potatoes. Sprinkle with parsley and serve with cooking juices.

*Serves 6*

## Chicken with Artichokes

Marinated artichoke hearts are available from delicatessens and some supermarkets. If they are unavailable use canned artichokes instead and marinate them yourself in a mixture of olive oil, lemon juice and fresh or dried herbs of your choice.

1 tblspn olive oil

60g (2oz) butter

1.5kg (3lb) chicken pieces

salt

freshly ground black pepper

170g (5¹/₂oz) marinated artichoke hearts, drained and quartered

6 tblspn white wine

12 pitted black olives

90ml (3fl oz) double cream

chopped fresh parsley, to serve

**1** Heat oil and butter in a large, flameproof casserole and when foam subsides, add chicken, skin side down. Sprinkle with salt and black pepper to taste, cover and cook over moderate heat for 10 minutes each side, or until brown.

**2** Add artichokes, wine and olives, lower heat, cover and cook for 10 minutes or until chicken is tender. Transfer chicken, artichokes and olives to a serving platter and keep warm.

**3** Add cream to cooking liquid and simmer, stirring, until sauce reduces and thickens. Spoon sauce over chicken and sprinkle with parsley.

*Serves 4-6*

## Beef and Black Walnuts

2 tblspn olive oil

90g (3oz) butter

1kg (2lb) lean stewing steak, cubed

2 cloves garlic, crushed

2 large onions, sliced

250ml (8fl oz) beef stock

185ml (6fl oz) red wine

1 bay leaf

1 tblspn finely grated orange rind

salt

freshly ground black pepper

8 pickled walnuts

**1** Preheat oven to 180°C (350°F/ Gas 4). Heat oil and 60g (2oz) butter in a large, flameproof casserole and cook steak over moderate heat until brown on all sides. Remove and set aside.

**2** Add garlic and onions to casserole and cook, stirring, until onions are golden. Return meat to casserole. Add stock, wine, bay leaf and orange rind. Season with salt and black pepper.

**3** Cover and bake for 1¹/₂ hours or until meat is tender. Stir in walnuts and remaining butter and cook for 3-4 minutes longer or until heated through.

*Serves 6*

## Caillettes

This is the Niçoise version of beef or veal olives. They are delicious served with the traditional accompaniments of mashed potatoes and boiled carrots and peas.

125g (4oz) pancetta or ham, chopped

2 cloves garlic, finely chopped

2 tblspn chopped fresh parsley

pinch chopped fresh thyme leaves

12 thin slices beef silverside or rump steak

1 tblspn drained capers

6 canned anchovy fillets, drained and finely chopped

2 hard-boiled eggs, chopped

2 tblspn olive oil

2 onions, sliced

1 stalk celery, sliced

1-1.2 litres (1³/₄-2pt) beef stock

**1** Combine pancetta or ham, garlic, parsley and thyme. Divide mixture evenly between beef slices and spread along one long edge of each slice, top with capers, anchovies and eggs and roll up, tucking ends in, to encase the filling. Tie securely with string to make neat shapes.

**2** Heat oil in a flameproof casserole and cook rolls, in batches, over moderate heat until brown on all sides. Remove and set aside.

**3** Add onions and celery to pan and cook, stirring, until onions are soft and golden. Return rolls to pan and add enough stock to half cover rolls. Cover and simmer gently, turning occasionally, for 1¹/₂ hours or until meat is tender.

*Serves 6*

*Braised Rolled Shoulder of Lamb*

## Peppered Chicken

*3 tblspn olive oil*

*1 clove garlic, crushed*

*1 tblspn green peppercorns, drained*

*2 red or green peppers, diced*

*6-8 chicken pieces*

*plain flour*

*1 small onion, finely chopped*

*185ml (6fl oz) dry white wine*

*2 tblspn tomato purée*

**1** Heat 1 tablespoon oil in a flameproof casserole and cook garlic, green peppercorns and red or green peppers over moderate heat, stirring, for 3-4 minutes. Remove and set aside.

**2** Toss chicken in flour to coat. Heat remaining oil in casserole and cook chicken, in batches, until golden. Drain off excess oil. Return chicken to casserole, add onion, wine and tomato purée and bring to the boil. Cover and simmer for 20 minutes. Return pepper mixture to casserole and simmer for 10 minutes or until chicken is tender.

*Serves 4*

## Beef and Prune Casserole

*125g (4oz) pitted prunes*

*600ml (1pt) hot beef stock*

*1kg (2lb) lean stewing steak, cut into 5cm (2in) cubes*

*2 tblspn seasoned flour*

*60g (2oz) butter*

*1 tblspn olive oil*

*1 tblspn tomato purée*

*2 bay leaves*

*2 firm-ripe tomatoes, peeled, seeded and quartered*

**1** Soak prunes in stock for 30 minutes. Toss steak in flour. Heat butter and oil in a flameproof casserole and cook beef, in batches, over moderate heat until brown. Return meat to casserole.

**2** Drain prunes, reserving stock. Add stock to beef and bring to the boil. Simmer for 15 minutes or until liquid reduces slightly.

**3** Chop six prunes and add to beef with tomato purée and bay leaves. Cover and simmer gently for 1³/₄ hours or until beef is tender. Add tomatoes and remaining whole prunes, cover and simmer for 15 minutes longer.

*Serves 6*

## Chicken with Dumplings

*6-8 chicken pieces*

*salt*

*4 tblspn plain flour*

*60g (2oz) butter*

*1 small onion, chopped*

*2 stalks celery with leaves, sliced*

*2 carrots, sliced*

*8-10 pickling onions or small white onions, peeled*

*2-3 tblspn chopped fresh parsley*

*1 bay leaf*

*375-500ml (12-16fl oz) hot chicken stock*

*185g (6oz) green peas, optional*

*freshly ground black pepper*

*freshly squeezed lemon juice*

**Parsley Dumplings**

*185g (6oz) plain flour*

*2 tspn baking powder*

*³/₄ tspn salt*

*1 tblspn finely chopped fresh parsley*

*pinch dried thyme*

*60g (2oz) butter*

*155-185ml (5-6fl oz) milk*

**1** Sprinkle chicken with salt and dust with half the flour. Melt butter in a flameproof casserole, add chicken and chopped onion and cook, turning occasionally, over moderate heat until chicken is golden. Stir in remaining flour and cook for 2-3 minutes longer.

**2** Add celery, carrots, whole onions, parsley and bay leaf to casserole. Pour over enough stock to just cover mixture and bring to the boil, stirring. Cover and simmer for 25 minutes. Add peas (if using), cover and cook for 10 minutes or until chicken is tender. Season to taste with salt, black pepper and lemon juice.

**3** To make dumplings, sift flour, baking powder and salt into a bowl, stir in parsley and thyme. Rub in butter, then stir in enough milk to make a moist dough.

**4** Shape tablespoons of dough into rounds and drop onto simmering chicken, ensuring they rest on chicken and do not sink into the sauce. Cover tightly and simmer, undisturbed, for 15 minutes.

*Serves 6*

## Lamb Goulash

*60g (2oz) butter*

*1kg (2lb) lamb neck chops, trimmed of visible fat*

*3 large onions, sliced*

*2 tblspn sweet paprika*

*1 tblspn plain flour*

*185ml (6fl oz) red wine or stock*

*2 x 440g (14oz) cans tomatoes, drained and chopped*

*salt*

*freshly ground black pepper*

*200g (6¹/₂oz) natural yogurt*

*1 tblspn chopped fresh parsley*

**1** Preheat oven to 180°C (350°F/Gas 4). Melt butter in a flameproof casserole and cook chops, in batches, over moderate heat until brown on both sides. Remove and set aside.

**2** Add onions to casserole and cook, stirring, for 8 minutes or until golden. Stir in paprika and flour. Gradually stir in wine or stock and mix until smooth. Add tomatoes and season to taste. Return chops to casserole, cover and bake for 1¹/₄ hours or until chops are tender.

**3** Stir in yogurt and heat, without boiling, for 4-5 minutes or until heated through. Sprinkle with parsley and serve.

*Serves 4*

*Peppered Chicken*

*Swedish Shanks with Dill*

## Italian Braised Shanks

6 lamb shanks (knuckles), trimmed of visible fat, (see Kitchen Tip, this page)

salt

freshly ground black pepper

1 tblspn chopped fresh oregano or 1 tspn dried

plain flour

90ml (3fl oz) olive oil

2 tspn finely grated lemon rind

1 onion, chopped

125g (4oz) chopped celery

2 small carrots, chopped

1 clove garlic, crushed

2 firm-ripe tomatoes, peeled, seeded and quartered

185ml (6fl oz) red wine

185ml (6fl oz) beef stock

1 tblspn plain flour blended with 2 tspn soft butter

**1** Season lamb with salt, black pepper and oregano and dust with flour. Heat oil in a flameproof casserole and cook lamb, in batches, over moderate heat until brown. Remove lamb, sprinkle with lemon rind and set aside.

**2** Add onion, celery, carrots and garlic to casserole and cook, stirring, over moderate heat for 5 minutes. Add tomatoes, wine and stock, bring to the boil and boil, stirring, for 3-5 minutes. Return lamb to casserole, cover and bake for 1½ hours or until lamb is tender.

**3** Transfer lamb to a serving platter and keep warm. Gradually stir flour mixture into sauce and cook over moderate heat, stirring, until sauce boils and thickens. Spoon sauce over lamb.

*Serves 6*

## Swedish Shanks with Dill

1 tblspn vegetable oil

60g (2oz) butter

6 lamb shanks (knuckles), trimmed of visible fat, (see Kitchen Tip, this page)

1 large onion, chopped

375ml (12fl oz) dry white wine

125ml (4fl oz) beef stock

1 bay leaf

2 tblspn plain flour

3 tblspn chopped fresh dill or 2 tspn dried

250g (8oz) sour cream

**1** Heat oil and half the butter in a flameproof casserole and cook lamb over moderate heat until brown. Remove and set aside.

**2** Add onion to casserole and cook, stirring, until golden. Add wine and stock and bring to the boil. Return shanks to casserole. Add bay leaf, cover and simmer for 1½-2 hours or until lamb is tender. Remove lamb and keep warm. Strain cooking liquid.

**3** Melt remaining butter in the casserole, stir in flour and cook over moderate heat for 1 minute. Slowly stir in stock and cook, stirring constantly, until sauce boils and thickens. Add dill and sour cream and season to taste. Return lamb to casserole and cook, without boiling, for 5 minutes.

*Serves 6*

**Kitchen Tip**
When buying lamb shanks (knuckles), ask the butcher to cut the nobbly ends off, but keep them to simmer with the shanks (knuckles) to give a flavoursome thick gravy. Discard nobbly ends before serving shanks.

# Oxtail Casserole

2 carrots, thinly sliced

2 onions, sliced

1 large clove garlic, crushed

1 bouquet garni

2 oxtails, cut into pieces

125g (4oz) bacon or ham, diced

1 pig's trotter

500ml (16fl oz) white wine

500ml (16fl oz) beef stock

salt

freshly ground black pepper

45g (1¹/₂oz) butter

12 pickling onions or small white onions, peeled, blanched in boiling water and drained

2-3 carrots, thickly sliced

4 lettuce hearts

chopped fresh parsley, to serve

**1** Preheat oven to 180°C (350°F/ Gas 4). Combine thinly sliced carrots, sliced onions, garlic and bouquet garni in a large casserole. Top with oxtails, bacon or ham and pig's trotter and bake, uncovered, for 30 minutes or until browned.

**2** Lower oven temperature to 150°C (300°F/Gas 2). Pour wine and stock over oxtails and season to taste with salt and black pepper. Cover and bake for 3 hours or until oxtails are tender.

**3** Using a slotted spoon, remove oxtails and keep warm. Strain cooking liquid and discard pig's trotter, vegetables and bouquet garni. Skim off excess fat, then return oxtails and stock to a clean casserole.

**4** Melt butter in a large frying pan and cook blanched onions, thickly sliced carrots and lettuce over moderate heat for 3-4 minutes. Add to casserole, cover and bake for 30 minutes longer or until vegetables are tender. Sprinkle with parsley and serve.

*Serves 6*

# Osso Bucco

In Italian Osso Bucco literally means 'bone with a hole'. Ask for the hind shins – they're meatier and more tender than those from the front.

1.2kg (2¹/₂lb) veal shin, cut crosswise into thick slices

60g (2oz) seasoned flour

60g (2oz) butter

3 carrots, chopped

3 stalks celery, chopped

1 large onion, chopped

2 large cloves garlic, crushed

250ml (8fl oz) beef stock

250mL (8 fl oz) white wine

3 firm-ripe tomatoes, peeled, seeded and chopped

1 sprig fresh rosemary leaves or ¹/₂ tspn dried

4 tblspn finely chopped fresh parsley

2-3 tspn finely grated lemon rind

1 tspn finely chopped garlic

**1** Wipe veal pieces with a damp paper towel to remove any bone dust, then coat with seasoned flour. Melt butter in a flameproof casserole and cook veal, in batches, over moderate heat until brown on both sides. Remove veal and set aside.

**2** Add carrots, celery, onion and 2 cloves garlic to casserole and cook, stirring, until vegetables are soft and golden. Return veal to casserole standing pieces upright so the marrow doesn't fall out during cooking. Add stock, wine, tomatoes and rosemary and season to taste.

**3** Bring to the boil, then lower heat, cover and simmer gently for 1¹/₂ hours or until meat is tender. Combine parsley, lemon rind and remaining garlic, sprinkle over veal and serve.

*Serves 4-6*

*Oxtail Casserole*

## Coq au Vin

500ml (16fl oz) red wine

375ml (12fl oz) chicken stock

2 bay leaves

1 sprig fresh thyme, or 1/4 tspn dried

1 clove garlic, crushed

250g (8oz) button mushrooms, stems removed

2 tblspn olive oil

60g (2oz) butter

125g (4oz) bacon rashers, diced

12 pickling onions or small white onions, peeled

1.5kg (3lb) chicken, cut into pieces

60ml (2fl oz) brandy

1 bouquet garni

1 clove garlic, peeled

salt

freshly ground black pepper

chopped fresh parsley, to serve

bread shapes fried in butter and oil, for garnish, optional

**1** Bring wine, stock, bay leaves, thyme and crushed garlic to the boil in a large saucepan. Boil briskly until liquid reduces by half. Add mushrooms and simmer for 5 minutes. Using a slotted spoon remove mushrooms. Reserve mushrooms and stock.

**2** Heat oil and half the butter in a large, flameproof casserole or heavy saucepan and cook bacon over moderate heat until fat runs. Add onions and sauté until golden. Add chicken pieces, skin side down, and cook, turning once, until golden on all sides.

**3** Heat brandy, ignite and pour over chicken. When flames subside, add bouquet garni, remaining garlic and reserved stock. Bring to simmering, cover and simmer gently for 40 minutes or until chicken is tender. Add mushrooms and simmer for 5 minutes longer.

**4** Transfer chicken, mushrooms, onions and bacon to a serving platter and keep warm. Strain sauce, season to taste with salt

and black pepper and stir in remaining butter. Pour sauce over chicken, sprinkle with parsley, garnish with fried bread shapes (if using) and serve.

*Serves 4*

## Oriental Spareribs

1.5kg (3lb) pork spareribs

3 tblspn vegetable oil

100ml (3 1/2fl oz) soy sauce

100ml (3 1/2fl oz) water

2 tblspn hoisin sauce

1 tspn sugar

4 slices fresh ginger, shredded

2 onions, finely sliced

100ml (3 1/2fl oz) dry sherry

salt

freshly ground white pepper

100ml (3 1/2fl oz) chicken stock

**1** Blanch spareribs in a large saucepan of boiling water for 5 minutes, drain and pat dry on paper towels. Preheat oven to 150°C (300°F/Gas 2).

**2** Heat oil in a flameproof casserole and stir fry ribs over moderate heat for 5 minutes or until brown. Add soy sauce, water, hoisin sauce, sugar, ginger and onions to casserole and cook, stirring, until ribs are well-coated with mixture. Cover and bake for 20 minutes.

**3** Add sherry to casserole and season to taste with salt and white pepper. Bake, covered, for 40 minutes, stirring once. Increase oven temperature to 220°C (425°F/ Gas 7).

**4** Arrange ribs in a single layer in a shallow ovenproof dish and bake for 12-15 minutes or until ribs are crisp and golden. Transfer to a serving platter and keep warm.

**5** Add stock to juices in casserole and stir over moderate heat for 2-3 minutes or until sauce boils and thickens. Serve sauce with ribs.

*Serves 4-6*

## Greek Lemon Chicken

For a complete meal serve with boiled rice and a steamed green vegetable such as beans or courgettes.

2-3 tblspn freshly squeezed lemon juice

pinch ground cloves

1/2 tspn ground cinnamon

salt

freshly ground black pepper

6-8 chicken pieces

125ml (4fl oz) olive oil

6 plum (egg or Italian) tomatoes, peeled and chopped

2 tblspn tomato purée

600ml (1pt) hot water

**1** Combine lemon juice, cloves, cinnamon and salt and black pepper to taste. Rub mixture over chicken pieces.

**2** Heat oil in a large saucepan and cook chicken over moderate heat until brown on all sides. Remove from pan and keep warm.

**3** Stir tomatoes and tomato purée into pan juices, then gradually stir in water and bring to simmering. Cook over low heat until tomatoes are mushy and sauce thickens.

**4** Return chicken to pan, cover and simmer for 30 minutes or until chicken is tender.

*Serves 4-6*

*Coq au Vin*

# FAVOURITE FAMILY ROASTS

*New-look roast pork has its crackling cooked separately to reduce the fat. Vegetables roasted with these meats add fibre and nutrition — and help save on the washing up! Look for ideas here suitable for casual weekend meals – when you've got time to relax over the cooking.*

## Loin of Pork Provençal

1.5-2kg (3-4lb) loin of pork, boned, rind removed and reserved

1 large clove garlic, cut into 4-5 slivers

1/2 tspn finely grated lemon rind

4 tblspn chopped fresh parsley

3-4 sprigs fresh thyme, or 1/2 tspn dried

salt

freshly ground black pepper

185ml (6fl oz) dry white or red wine

1 bay leaf, crushed

3 tblspn dried breadcrumbs

**1** Unroll pork and place fat side down. Scatter with garlic, lemon rind and half each of the parsley and thyme. Season to taste. Reroll and tie into a neat shape. Place pork in a deep non-reactive dish, add wine, bay leaf and remaining thyme, cover and marinate in the refrigerator for 2-3 hours.

**2** Preheat oven to 200°C (400°F/ Gas 6). Place rind, fat side down and cut into strips. Rub with salt and bake for 30 minutes or until puffed and crisp. Set aside.

**3** Lower oven temperature to 180°C (350°F/Gas 4). Place pork and marinade in a casserole or baking dish, cover with lid or foil and bake, basting occasionally, for 1½ hours, adding a little water if marinade evaporates.

**4** Combine breadcrumbs and remaining parsley, press onto pork and bake, uncovered, for 30 minutes, basting every 10 minutes, until a golden crust forms. Cover and stand for 10-15 minutes. Just prior to serving reheat crackling and serve with pork.

*Serves 6*

## Herbed Lamb with Vegetables

1.75kg (3½lb) leg of lamb

1 sprig fresh rosemary

salt

freshly ground black pepper

750g (1½lb) potatoes, thickly sliced

2 onions, thinly sliced

3 firm-ripe tomatoes, sliced

1 tblspn fresh oregano leaves or 1 tspn dried

1 medium aubergine or 4 long, narrow ones, thickly sliced

1 red or green pepper, cut into strips

3-4 tblspn chopped mixed fresh herbs such as parsley, chervil, oregano

**1** Preheat oven to 220°C (425°F/ Gas 7). Make 5-6 slits in surface of lamb and insert 2-3 rosemary leaves in each. Season to taste.

**2** Place lamb, fat side up, in a roasting tin. Surround with potatoes and onions, then top with tomatoes and sprinkle with oregano. Bake for 15 minutes. Lower oven temperature to 180°C (350°F/Gas 4), baste lamb with pan juices and bake for 1 hour.

**3** Turn lamb over, add aubergine and red or green pepper strips to tin and bake, turning lamb and basting occasionally, for 45-60 minutes longer, or until lamb is cooked to your liking.

**4** Drain excess fat from tin sprinkle vegetables with herbs and toss to combine.

*Serves 8*

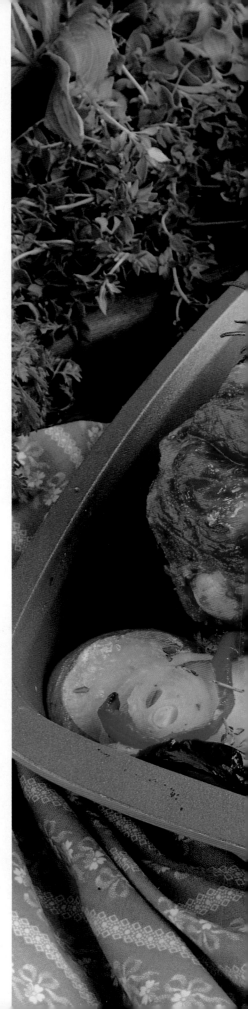

*Herbed Lamb with Vegetables*

## Cold Beef Provençal

A magnificent idea for special occasions. You can use a short fillet from the rump to serve 6-8 people or two fillets for a buffet.

1kg (2lb) fillet of beef, trimmed of excess fat

freshly ground black pepper

1 tblspn olive oil

30g (1oz) butter

60ml (2fl oz) brandy

250g (8oz) green beans, trimmed

250g (8oz) small courgettes or baby squash, thickly sliced

500g (1lb) firm-ripe tomatoes, peeled and quartered

60g (2oz) pitted black olives

1 tblspn chopped mixed fresh herbs such as parsley, basil, oregano, fresh sprigs tarragon, for garnish

**Green Herb Vinaigrette**

170ml (5¹/₂fl oz) virgin olive oil

60ml (2fl oz) white or red wine vinegar

1 tspn French mustard

1 clove garlic, crushed

3 tblspn finely chopped mixed fresh herbs, such as chives, parsley, oregano, tarragon, basil

salt

freshly ground black pepper

**1** Preheat oven to 250°C (500°F/ Gas 9). Sprinkle fillet with black pepper. Heat oil and butter in a large, heavy-based frying pan and cook beef over moderate heat until brown on all sides.

**2** Heat brandy and ignite, then pour over beef and shake pan until flames subside. Transfer beef and juices to a roasting tin, lower oven temperature to 220°C (425°F/ Gas 7) and bake for 25 minutes. Cool completely.

**3** To make vinaigrette, combine oil, vinegar, mustard, garlic, herbs and salt and black pepper to taste in a screwtop jar. Shake well to combine.

**4** Boil, steam or microwave beans and courgettes or squash, separately, until they just change colour and are just tender, drain and toss with tomatoes and olives. Add most of the vinaigrette and toss to combine.

**5** Cut beef into 1cm (¹/₂in) thick slices and arrange with vegetables on a serving platter. Sprinkle beef with remaining vinaigrette and garnish with herbs.

*Serves 8*

## Lamb with Beans and Tomatoes

You've a choice of using dried white beans in the French manner, or when fresh borlotti beans are in season they are perfect to use for this dish.

500g (1lb) dried haricot beans or fresh borlotti beans

2 large onions, quartered

1 bouquet garni

2 cloves garlic

1 tspn salt

few black peppercorns

1.75kg (3¹/₂lb) leg of lamb, trimmed of excess fat

salt

freshly ground black pepper

250ml (8fl oz) water

60g (2oz) butter

4 spring onions or 1 small onion, chopped

2 large firm-ripe tomatoes, peeled and diced

2 tblspn chopped fresh parsley

**1** Place dried beans (if using) in a large bowl, pour over enough cold water to cover and soak overnight. Drain. Place soaked or fresh beans in a large saucepan and pour over enough cold water to cover. Add quartered onions, bouquet garni, 1 clove garlic, salt and black peppercorns and slowly bring to the boil. Skim off any scum that forms during cooking, reduce heat, cover and simmer gently until beans are just tender – 1¹/₂-2 hours for dried, 45-60 minutes for fresh beans. Drain and set aside.

**2** Preheat oven to 190°C (375°F/ Gas 5). Cut remaining garlic into slivers. Using a small sharp knife make slits over the surface of the lamb and insert garlic. Sprinkle with salt and black pepper to taste and place on a rack in a roasting tin. Add water and half the butter to tin and bake, basting every 15 minutes, for 1¹/₂ hours or until lamb is cooked to your liking.

**3** Melt remaining butter in a frying pan and cook spring onions or onion over low heat until soft. Add tomatoes, cooked beans and 125ml (4fl oz) baking juices, cover and simmer for 20 minutes. Sprinkle with parsley and serve with lamb. Strain any remaining pan juices and serve separately.

*Serves 6*

## Roast Rosemary Chicken

3 cloves garlic

1 sprig fresh rosemary leaves, chopped or 1 tspn dried

1.5kg (3lb) chicken

salt

freshy ground black pepper

4 tblspn olive oil

1-2 tblspn water or white wine

**1** Preheat oven to 190°C (375°F/ Gas 5). Place garlic and half the rosemary in cavity of bird and sprinkle with salt and black pepper to taste. Rub skin all over with half the oil, sprinkle with remaining rosemary and place in a roasting tin or flameproof casserole.

**2** Add remaining oil to tin or casserole, cover with foil or lid and bake, turning and basting every 15 minutes, for 1 hour. Turn chicken breast side up and bake, uncovered, for 20 minutes longer, or until chicken is tender and skin is brown and crisp.

**3** Transfer bird to a serving dish and keep warm. Discard all but 1 tablespoon fat from cooking juices, add water or wine to pan juices and simmer over high heat, stirring, for 2 minutes. Spoon juices over chicken and serve immediately.

*Serves 4-6*

*Cold Beef Provençal*

# Favourite Roast Chicken

1.5kg (3lb) chicken

125g (4oz) streaky bacon rashers

30g (1oz) soft butter

1 tblspn plain flour

### Chicken Stock

250g (8oz) chicken giblets and neck

1 small unpeeled onion, quartered

1 sprig each fresh thyme and parsley

1 small bay leaf

3-4 black peppercorns

600ml (1pt) water

### Lemon and Parsley Stuffing

60g (2oz) breadcrumbs, made from stale bread

2-3 tspn finely grated lemon rind

1 tspn chopped fresh thyme or 1/4 tspn dried

1 tspn chopped fresh marjoram or 1/4 tspn dried

salt

freshly ground black pepper

1-2 tblspn freshly squeezed lemon juice

60g (2oz) butter, melted

1 small egg, beaten, optional

**1** To make stock, place giblets, neck, onion, herbs, black peppercorns and water in a saucepan and bring to the boil. Lower heat, cover and simmer gently for at least 1 hour. Strain stock and set aside.

**2** Preheat oven to 200°C (400°F/ Gas 6). To make stuffing, place breadcrumbs, lemon rind, herbs and salt and black pepper to taste in a bowl and mix to combine. Add lemon juice, butter and egg (if using) and mix to combine.

**3** Rinse chicken and wipe dry. Loosely fill cavity with stuffing, tuck wings under body and tie bird into a neat shape. Cover breast with bacon and rub legs with butter.

**4** Place bird in a roasting tin or flameproof casserole, cover with foil or lid and bake for 1 hour. Remove from oven, remove bacon and reserve. Baste chicken and

bake, uncovered, for 15-30 minutes longer or until tender and golden. Transfer chicken and bacon to a serving platter and keep warm.

**5** To make gravy, discard all but 1 tablespoon fat from cooking juices, stir in flour and cook over moderate heat for 2-3 minutes or until brown. Remove from heat and stir in 375-440ml (12-14fl oz) stock. Cook over moderate heat, stirring constantly, until gravy boils and thickens. Season to taste.

*Serves 4-6*

# Chicken Bonne Femme

1.5kg (3lb) chicken

salt

freshly ground black pepper

125g (4oz) sausage meat

1 chicken liver, chopped, optional

4-5 tblspn breadcrumbs, made from stale bread

2 tblspn chopped fresh parsley

1-2 fresh sage leaves, chopped, or pinch dried

30g (1oz) butter

4 onions, quartered

1 rasher streaky bacon, chopped

2 potatoes, cubed

**1** Rinse chicken and wipe dry. Season cavity with salt and black pepper. Combine sausage meat, chicken liver (if using), breadcrumbs, parsley and sage in a bowl. Loosely fill cavity of chicken with mixture. Tuck wings under body and tie bird into a neat shape.

**2** Heat butter in a flameproof casserole, add chicken, onions, bacon and potatoes, cover and cook over low heat, turning chicken frequently, for 1-1¼ hours or until chicken is tender and juices run clear when thigh is pierced.

*Serves 4-6*

*Favourite Roast Chicken*

*Roast Pork with Crackling*

## Roast Pork with Crackling

*1 leg of pork, trimmed of excess fat, rind removed and reserved*

*2 tspn coarsely crushed black peppercorns*

*salt*

*1 tblspn plain flour*

*250ml (8fl oz) chicken stock*

*125ml (4fl oz) white wine*

*freshly ground black pepper*

*sliced apples fried in butter or applesauce, to serve*

**1** Preheat oven to 180°C (350°F/ Gas 4). Weigh pork to calculate cooking time. Press peppercorns over surface of pork and place on a rack in a roasting tin. Pour in water to fill tin to a level of 2cm (³/₄in).

**2** Bake pork for 30 minutes per 500g (1lb), plus an extra 30 minutes, or until a meat thermometer inserted into the thickest part registers 76°C (170°F). Pork is cooked when juices run clear when the thickest part of muscle is pierced with a skewer. Place pork on a serving dish, cover and keep warm. Increase oven temperature to 250°C (500°F/Gas 9).

**3** Place pork rind in a roasting tin, rub lightly with salt and bake for 20 minutes or until skin is puffed and crisp. Break crackling into pieces.

**4** To make gravy, discard all but 1 tablespoon fat from cooking juices, stir in flour and cook over moderate heat for 2-3 minutes or until brown. Remove pan from heat and stir in stock and wine. Return to heat and cook, stirring constantly, until gravy boils and thickens. Season to taste. Serve pork with crackling, gravy and apples or applesauce.

*Serves 8*

## Lamb Boulangère

1.75kg (3¹/₂lb) leg of lamb

2 cloves garlic, cut into slivers

salt

freshly ground black pepper

8 potatoes, peeled and sliced

1 large onion, finely sliced or chopped

375ml (12fl oz) dry white wine

250ml (8fl oz) stock or water

2 tblspn chopped fresh parsley or mint

**1** Preheat oven to 200°C (400°F/ Gas 6). Trim lamb of excess fat and using a small sharp knife make slits over surface. Insert garlic into slits and sprinkle lightly with salt and black pepper to taste.

**2** Arrange potatoes and onion in a well-buttered roasting tin and sprinkle with salt and black pepper to taste. Add wine and stock or water. Place lamb on a rack in tin and bake for 20 minutes.

**3** Lower oven temperature to 180°C (350°F/Gas 4) and bake, adding a little extra stock to potatoes if needed, for 1-1¹/₄ hours longer, or until liquid is absorbed, potatoes are tender and lamb is cooked to your liking.

**4** Place lamb on a serving platter, surround with potatoes and sprinkle with parsley or mint.

*Serves 6-8*

## Rack of Lamb for Two

1 rack of lamb containing 6 cutlets, trimmed of excess fat

1 clove garlic, cut into 6 slivers

1 sprig fresh thyme or pinch dried

salt

freshly ground black pepper

60ml (2fl oz) water or wine

2 carrots, cut into thin strips

6 baby new potatoes, parboiled for 10 minutes and drained

1 tblspn breadcrumbs, made from stale bread

1 tblspn olive or vegetable oil

1 firm-ripe tomato, halved

1-2 tblspn chopped fresh parsley

125ml (4fl oz) dry white or red wine

2 tspn butter

**1** Preheat oven to 200°C (400°F/ Gas 6). Make six slits in flesh of lamb and insert garlic. Sprinkle lamb with thyme and season to taste. Place in a roasting tin, add 60ml (2fl oz) water or wine, carrots and potatoes and bake for 15 minutes.

**2** Sauté breadcrumbs in hot oil, spoon over tomato halves and place in dish with lamb. Bake for 10 minutes longer or until lamb is cooked to your liking.

**3** Transfer lamb and vegetables to a serving platter, sprinkle with parsley and keep warm. Add 125ml (4fl oz) wine to juices in tin and simmer, stirring, until sauce thickens. Stir in butter, strain and serve with lamb.

*Serves 2*

## Orange and Honey Chicken

1.5kg (3lb) chicken

salt

freshly ground black pepper

60g (2oz) butter

2 oranges, peeled, all white pith removed

2 stalks celery, chopped

1 sprig fresh parsley

125ml (4fl oz) dry white wine or vermouth

125ml (4fl oz) freshly squeezed orange juice

125ml (4fl oz) water

4 tblspn honey

**1** Preheat oven to 190°C (375°F/ Gas 5). Rinse chicken and pat dry with paper towels. Season cavity with salt and black pepper and fill with half the butter, 1 whole orange, the celery and parsley. Rub skin with remaining butter.

**2** Place bird in a roasting tin, add wine or vermouth, orange juice and water, cover breast loosely with aluminium foil and bake for 45 minutes. Remove foil, baste with pan juices, drizzle with honey and bake for 30 minutes longer or until chicken is tender and cooked

through. Transfer to a serving platter, cover and keep warm.

**3** To make sauce, skim excess fat from cooking juices and strain liquid into a small saucepan. Bring to the boil, lower heat and simmer until liquid reduces and thickens. Season to taste with salt and black pepper. Cut remaining orange into segments or slices and use to garnish chicken. Serve with sauce.

*Serves 4-6*

## Pork with Prunes and Anchovies

2kg (4lb) loin of pork, boned and rind removed

12 whole almonds

12 pitted dessert prunes

12 canned anchovy fillets, drained

freshly ground black pepper

1 tblspn plain flour

250ml (8fl oz) chicken stock or water

salt

**1** Trim excess fat from pork, unroll and place, fat side down. Place an almond in each prune, wrap with an anchovy and place prunes in a line along centre of loin. Season to taste with black pepper. Reroll and tie pork into a neat shape.

**2** Preheat oven to 180°C (350°F/ Gas 4). Place pork on a rack in a roasting tin, add 125ml (4fl oz) water to tin and bake for 2 hours or until juices run clear when thickest part of meat is pierced with a skewer. Place pork on a serving platter, cover and keep warm.

**3** To make gravy, discard all but 1 tablespoon fat from cooking juices, stir in flour and cook over moderate heat for 2-3 minutes or until brown. Remove from heat and gradually stir in stock or water. Cook over moderate heat, stirring constantly, until gravy boils and thickens. Season with salt and black pepper and serve with pork.

*Serves 6-8*

*Lamb Boulangère*

# Skewers, Sautes, Grills & Stir Fries

*When time is of the essence use these ideas to prepare tasty meals that are sure to please. Choose from flavoursome international favourites such as Veal Scallopine, Chop Suey, Indian-influenced lamb kebabs and Mediterranean-style chicken.*

## Spicy Inidan Kebabs

A northern Indian favourite.

750g (1¹/₂lb) lean boneless lamb, cut into 2.5cm (1in) cubes

2-3 tblspn freshly squeezed lemon juice

140g (4¹/₂oz) natural yogurt

2 cloves garlic, chopped

1 tspn freshly ground black pepper

1 tspn ground turmeric

¹/₂ tspn ground cumin

¹/₂ tspn salt

1 tblspn vinegar

1 large red onion, cut into thin wedges

1 green or red pepper, cut into 2.5cm (1in) squares

1 lemon, quartered, for garnish

pitta or naan bread and salad, to serve

**1** Place lamb and lemon juice in a bowl and toss to combine. Place yogurt, garlic, spices, vinegar and half the onion in a blender or food processor and process until smooth. Spoon mixture over lamb, toss to coat, cover and marinate in the refrigerator overnight.

**2** Drain lamb and thread onto lightly oiled skewers, alternately, with green or red pepper and remaining onion wedges. Cook under a preheated medium grill or on a barbecue, turning frequently, for 8-10 minutes or until lamb is tender. Garnish with lemon quarters and serve with pitta or naan bread and salad.

*Serves 6*

## Grilled Chicken Diavola

60g (2oz) butter, melted

3 tblspn olive oil

1 small dried red chilli, seeded and crushed

1 small onion, grated

2 tblspn chopped fresh parsley

1 large clove garlic, crushed

1.5kg (3lb) chicken pieces

1 tspn salt

1 lemon, cut into wedges, to serve

**1** Combine butter, oil and chilli and set aside. Combine onion, parsley and garlic, add 1 tablespoon of the butter mixture and stir to make a paste.

**2** Brush chicken with some of the butter mixture and sprinkle with salt. Cook under a preheated medium grill, turning and basting frequently with remaining butter mixture, for 20-25 minutes or until chicken is tender.

**3** Press parsley paste onto skin of chicken pieces and grill for 2-3 minutes longer or until coating is golden. Serve immediately with lemon wedges.

*Serves 4*

*Spicy Indian Kebabs*

## Beef Birds

6 thin slices topside or rump steak, pounded thinly

salt

freshly ground black pepper

12 thin slices ham

1 small carrot, finely chopped

2 stalks celery, finely chopped

60g (2oz) plain flour

2 tblspn vegetable oil

60g (2oz) bacon, chopped

1 onion, finely chopped

1 clove garlic, finely chopped

125ml (4fl oz) dry white wine

440g (14oz) can tomatoes, undrained and mashed

1 bay leaf

1 whole clove

2 tblspn finely chopped parsley

**1** Cut each steak in half crosswise and season to taste, then top each piece with a slice of ham. Combine carrot and half the celery, sprinkle over ham and roll up to enclose the filling. Tie rolls securely and toss with flour to lightly coat.

**2** Heat oil in a flameproof casserole or saucepan large enough to fit rolls in one layer. Add bacon, onion, garlic and remaining celery and cook over moderate heat, stirring, for 1 minute. Add rolls and cook until brown on all sides.

**3** Add wine to pan and simmer until almost evaporated. Add tomatoes, bay leaf and clove and bring to the boil. Lower heat, cover and simmer gently for 1 hour or until meat is tender.

**4** Transfer rolls to a serving platter, remove strings and keep warm. Season tomato mixture with salt and black pepper to taste, then push through a sieve and spoon over rolls. Sprinkle with parsley and serve.

*Serves 6*

## Rosemary Chops

4 pork loin or rib chops, cut 2.5cm (1in) thick

3 cloves garlic, cut into slivers

1 tblspn olive oil

45g (1 1/2 oz) butter

375g (12oz) button mushrooms, sliced

1 clove garlic, crushed

1 sprig fresh rosemary or 1/2 tspn dried

8 baby new potatoes, boiled until just tender and drained

2 tblspn chopped fresh parsley

### Rosemary Marinade

90ml (3fl oz) olive oil

1 tspn salt

1/4 tspn freshly ground black pepper

1 bay leaf, crushed

1 sprig fresh rosemary or 1/2 tspn dried

**1** To make marinade, place oil, salt, black pepper, bay leaf and rosemary in a shallow dish and mix to combine. Cut small slits in the chops and insert slivers of garlic. Add chops to marinade, cover and marinate in the refrigerator, turning occasionally, for at least 3 hours.

**2** Drain chops and pat dry with paper towels. Heat 1 tablespoon oil in a large, heavy-based frying pan and cook chops over moderate heat for 2 minutes each side or until golden. Lower heat and cook, partially covered, for 4-5 minutes each side or until chops are cooked.

**3** Melt butter in a separate frying pan and sauté mushrooms, garlic and rosemary for 6 minutes. Add potatoes and stir fry until potatoes are heated through. Sprinkle with parsley and serve with chops.

*Serves 4*

## Tarragon Veal Cutlets

This dish can also be made using lamb cutlets, however the cooking will be a little shorter.

6 thick veal rib cutlets

3 tblspn plain flour

2 tblspn vegetable oil

30g (1oz) butter

2 tblspn chopped spring onions

125ml (4fl oz) dry white wine

2 tspn chopped fresh tarragon or 1/4 tspn dried

salt

freshly ground black pepper

125ml (4fl oz) double cream

**1** Toss cutlets in flour to lightly coat. Heat oil and butter in a large, heavy-based frying pan and cook cutlets over moderate heat for 3-4 minutes each side or until golden. Set aside.

**2** Add spring onions to pan and cook, stirring, for 5 minutes. Add wine and tarragon and simmer, stirring, for 3 minutes. Return cutlets to pan and season to taste with salt and black pepper. Cover and simmer gently for 20-25 minutes or until tender.

**3** Transfer cutlets to a serving plate and keep warm. Stir cream into pan juices and simmer until sauce reduces and thickens. Serve sauce spooned over cutlets.

*Serves 6*

## Lamb Romana

90g (3oz) breadcrumbs, made from stale bread

5-6 tblspn chopped fresh parsley

3 cloves garlic, crushed

2 tspn salt

1/4 tspn freshly ground black pepper

1.25kg (2 1/2lb) lean boneless lamb, cut into 3cm (1 1/4in) cubes

60ml (2fl oz) olive oil

Preheat oven to 180°C (350°F/ Gas 4). Combine breadcrumbs, parsley, garlic, salt and black pepper. Brush lamb with some oil and roll in crumb mixture to coat. Place lamb in a roasting tin, drizzle with remaining oil and bake for 30 minutes or until lamb is cooked and coating is golden.

*Serves 6*

## Chicken and Carrot Fricasee

This dish can be simmered in a heavy-based saucepan over low heat on the stove if you prefer not to use the oven.

60g (2oz) butter

1 bunch baby carrots, trimmed

2 onions, quartered

2 cloves garlic

1.5kg (3lb) chicken, cut into pieces

salt

freshly ground black pepper

1 sprig fresh thyme

1 sprig fresh parsley

1 bay leaf

250ml (8fl oz) dry white wine

250ml (8fl oz) chicken stock

315ml (10fl oz) double cream

1 tblspn wine vinegar

2 egg yolks

**1** Preheat oven to 180°C (350°F/ Gas 4). Melt butter in a large, flameproof casserole and sauté carrots, onions and garlic over moderate heat for 5 minutes or until golden. Remove carrots and set aside.

**2** Season chicken with salt and black pepper to taste, add to casserole and cook over moderate heat for 3-4 minutes each side or until brown. Add herbs, wine and stock, cover and bake for 20 minutes.

**3** Return carrots to casserole, cover and bake for 10-15 minutes longer or until carrots and chicken are tender. Transfer chicken and carrots to a serving dish and keep warm.

**4** Place cream, vinegar and egg yolks in a bowl and whisk to combine. Stir in a little of the hot cooking juices, then stir mixture back into casserole. Cook over low heat, stirring constantly without boiling, until sauce thickens. Pour sauce over chicken and carrots and serve.

*Serves 6*

## Chicken Chop Suey

This satisfying family dish takes just six minutes to cook.

2 boneless chicken breast fillets

2 boneless chicken thigh fillets

2 cloves garlic, crushed

1 tspn cornflour

1 tblspn soy sauce

1 tblspn dry sherry

6 dried Chinese mushrooms

2-3 tblspn vegetable oil

2 stalks celery, cut into matchsticks

6-8 spring onions, cut into short lengths

125g (4oz) broccoli, broken into small florets

125ml (4fl oz) chicken stock

1 tblspn oyster sauce

freshly ground black pepper

**1** Cut chicken into thin strips and place in a bowl. Add 1 clove garlic, cornflour, soy sauce and sherry, mix well and set aside. Place mushrooms in a bowl, pour over hot water to cover and set aside to soak for 15 minutes. Drain and cut into thin strips.

**2** Heat oil in a large frying pan or wok until hot, add remaining garlic and stir fry until golden, then discard. Add chicken mixture to pan and stir fry for 2 minutes or until it just changes colour.

**3** Add vegetables to pan and stir fry for 5 minutes or until chicken and vegetables are just tender. Combine stock, oyster sauce and black pepper to taste, add to pan and cook, stirring, until sauce thickens and boils. Serve immediately.

*Serves 6*

## Veal Scallopine

500g (1lb) veal or turkey escalopes, pounded thinly

seasoned flour

1 tblspn virgin olive oil

125ml (4fl oz) dry white wine

1 tblspn butter

1 tblspn balsamic vinegar

2 tblspn finely chopped fresh basil leaves or 1/2 tspn dried

salt

freshly ground black pepper

**1** Toss escalopes in flour to coat. Shake off any excess flour. Heat oil in a large, heavy-based frying pan and cook escalopes, a few at a time, over moderate heat for 2 minutes each side or until cooked and golden. Transfer to a serving platter and keep warm.

**2** Add wine to pan and simmer, stirring, over moderate heat to reduce slightly. Lower heat, add butter, vinegar and basil and cook until heated through. Season to taste with salt and black pepper. Spoon sauce over escalopes and serve immediately.

*Serves 4*

*Chicken and Carrot Fricasee*

## Chicken Mediterranean

1.5kg (3lb) chicken, halved

freshly ground black pepper

2 tblspn olive oil

1 tblspn butter, melted

4 large firm-ripe tomatoes, peeled, seeded and quartered

3 short, narrow cucumbers, peeled and diced

8 green olives

8 black olives

**1** Preheat oven to 220°C (425°F/ Gas 7). Pat chicken dry with paper towels and place, skin side up, in an ovenproof dish. Sprinkle with black pepper, drizzle with oil and bake, uncovered, for 25-30 minutes or until chicken is tender.

**2** Transfer chicken to a cutting board, cut into serving portions and arrange on a serving platter. Drizzle with butter and set aside to keep warm. Discard fat from cooking juices.

**3** Add tomatoes, cucumbers and olives to dish and bake for 5-10 minutes or until vegetables are hot. Spoon over chicken.

*Serves 4*

## Herbed Crumbed Cutlets

The cutlets can be coated the night before and stored in the refrigerator between sheets of greaseproof paper.

8 lamb cutlets, trimmed of excess fat

salt

freshly ground black pepper

90g (3oz) breadcrumbs, made from stale bread, or 125g (4oz) dried breadcrumbs

1 tblspn finely chopped fresh parsley

1 tspn finely chopped fresh thyme or 1/2 tspn dried

1 tspn finely chopped fresh marjoram or 1/2 tspn dried

1 tspn finely grated lemon rind

plain flour for dusting

2 eggs, beaten with 2 tspn water

2 tblspn vegetable oil

45g (11/2oz) butter

**1** Season cutlets with salt and black pepper. Combine bread-crumbs, herbs and lemon rind in a shallow dish. Toss cutlets in flour to coat, dip in egg mixture, then roll in crumb mixture to coat. Place cutlets on a plate lined with plastic food wrap and chill for 15 minutes.

**2** Heat oil and butter in a large, heavy-based frying pan and cook cutlets over moderate heat for 3-5 minutes each side or until tender and golden. Drain on paper towels and serve.

*Serves 4*

## Ham and Chicken Rolls

An easy microwavable dish.

4 boneless chicken breast fillets, pounded thinly

4 slices Gruyère cheese

4 thin slices ham

45g (11/2oz) butter

1 clove garlic, chopped

60g (2oz) dried breadcrumbs

2 tblspn freshly grated Parmesan cheese

1/2 tspn chopped fresh oregano, or pinch dried

**1** Top each fillet with a slice of cheese, then a slice of ham, folding or trimming slices so they do not extend beyond edge of chicken. Roll up fillets, folding ends in to enclose the filling, and secure with wooden toothpicks or cocktail sticks.

**2** Place butter in a small microwavable bowl and cook on HIGH (100%) for 45-55 seconds, then add garlic. Combine bread-crumbs, Parmesan cheese and oregano in a shallow dish. Dip rolls into butter mixture, then roll in crumb mixture to coat.

**3** Place rolls, like spokes on wheel with thicker ends to the outside, on a microwavable rack, cover with a paper towel and cook on HIGH (100%) for 3-5 minutes. Turn and cook for 4-6 minutes longer, or until chicken is tender and no longer pink. Cover loosely with foil and stand for 3 minutes before serving.

*Serves 4*

## Oven-fried Parmesan Chicken

60g (2oz) butter

3 tblspn plain flour

2 tblspn freshly grated Parmesan cheese

1 tspn salt

pinch curry powder

6-8 chicken pieces

250ml (8fl oz) chicken stock

125ml (4fl oz) double cream

freshly ground black pepper

**1** Preheat oven to 200°C (400°F/ Gas 6). Place butter in a roasting tin and heat in oven until melted. Combine 2 tablespoons flour, Parmesan cheese, salt and curry powder in a shallow dish.

**2** Remove tin from oven, roll chicken pieces in butter, then coat with flour mixture, pressing firmly. Arrange chicken, skin side down in tin. Bake, uncovered, for 20 minutes, turn over and bake for 10 minutes longer, or until chicken is cooked and golden. Transfer to a serving platter and keep warm.

**3** Discard excess fat from cooking juices. Place tin over low heat, stir in remaining flour and cook over moderate heat for 1 minute. Remove tin from heat and gradually stir in stock and cream. Cook over moderate heat, stirring constantly, until gravy boils and thickens. Season to taste with salt and black pepper and serve with chicken.

*Serves 4*

# THREE EASY MENUS FOR ENTERTAINING

*As the occasions arise, look to these menus for up to the minute meals that offer fresh food full of flavour with the minimum of fuss. Those recipes marked with an * are given here.*

---

### MENU ONE

* Chilled Avocado Soup

* Green Peppercorn Chicken

* Orange Rice

Mixed Green Salad

* Mangoes Jubilee

---

## Chilled Avocado Soup

This easy, quick-to-make, no-cook soup is the perfect way to make the most of avocados when they are at their cheapest.

2 firm-ripe avocados, stoned, peeled and chopped

1-2 tspn freshly squeezed lemon juice

200g (6¹/₂oz) natural yogurt

250ml (8fl oz) canned chicken consommé or chicken stock

60ml (2fl oz) double cream

³/₄ tspn Worcestershire sauce

4-6 drops Tabasco sauce

salt

freshly ground white pepper

3-4 tblspn chopped fresh coriander

**1** Place avocados in a blender or food processor, add lemon juice to taste, yogurt and 185ml (6fl oz) consommé or stock and process until smooth. Transfer to a bowl.

**2** Whisk in cream and enough remaining consommé to achieve the desired consistency. Season to taste with Worcestershire sauce, Tabasco sauce, salt and white pepper.

**3** Cover surface of soup with plastic food wrap and chill for 1 hour. Serve sprinkled with coriander.

*Serves 4*

## Green Peppercorn Chicken

1.5kg (3lb) chicken

60g (2oz) butter

2 tspn green peppercorns, drained and crushed

salt

375ml (12fl oz) dry white wine

**1** Remove neck from chicken and pat bird dry with paper towels.

**2** Preheat oven to 180°C (350°F/ Gas 4). Combine 30g (1oz) butter and peppercorns and set aside. Using your fingers gently loosen skin over breast of chicken, then push butter mixture gently between skin and flesh working it down into the thighs and smoothing evenly. Tuck wings under body and tie bird into a neat shape. Rub remaining butter over skin, sprinkle with salt and place in a casserole.

**3** Add 250ml (8fl oz) wine to casserole, cover breast loosely with aluminium foil and bake, turning bird and basting occasionally, for 1¹/₄ hours or until cooked. Transfer chicken to a serving platter and keep warm.

**4** Skim fat from cooking juices. Add remaining wine to cooking juices, then bring to the boil and boil until liquid reduces to 185ml (6fl oz). Strain sauce and serve with chicken.

*Serves 4-6*

## Orange Rice

45g (1¹/₂oz) butter

3-4 small stalks celery with leaves, finely chopped

2 tblspn finely chopped onion

375ml (12fl oz) water

2 tblspn finely grated orange rind

185ml (6fl oz) freshly squeezed orange juice

1 tspn salt

1 tspn chopped fresh thyme leaves or pinch dried

220g (7oz) uncooked long grain rice, washed

**1** Melt butter in a large saucepan and cook celery and onion over moderate heat, stirring, until onion is soft. Add water, orange rind, orange juice, salt and thyme and bring to the boil.

**2** Gradually stir rice into pan and return to boiling. Lower heat, cover and simmer gently for 20 minutes or until rice is tender and liquid absorbed. Fluff up rice with a fork and serve.

*Serves 4-6*

*Orange Rice, Green Peppercorn Chicken, Chilled Avocado Soup*

## Mangoes Jubilee

1 tblspn cornflour

2 tblspn water

440g (14oz) can sliced mangoes, drained, juice reserved

2 tblspn rum

vanilla ice cream, to serve

**1** Combine cornflour and water in a small saucepan and slowly stir in reserved mango juice. Cook over moderate heat, stirring constantly, until sauce boils and thickens. Stir in mango slices and cook gently until heated through.

**2** Heat rum, ignite and pour over sauce. Shake pan until flames subside, then turn fruit in sauce to glaze. Spoon mangoes and sauce over scoops of ice cream and serve immediately.

Serves 4

---

### MENU TWO

* Grilled Lamb Cutlets

* Carrots Vichy

* Potatoes with Sun-dried
Tomatoes

Steamed Green Beans

* Fruit Fool

---

## Grilled Lamb Cutlets

8 lamb cutlets, trimmed of excess fat

1 tspn fresh oregano leaves or 1/2 tspn dried

freshly ground black pepper

2 tblspn olive oil

**1** Season cutlets with oregano and black pepper to taste and brush with oil. Place on a plate and marinate at room temperature for 30 minutes.

**2** Cook cutlets under a preheated medium grill for 2 minutes each side to seal in juices, then cook for

1-2 minutes longer or until cooked to your liking. Serve immediately.

Serves 4

## Carrots Vichy

If using large carrots for this dish, peel and cut into strips or thin slices – young carrots can be left whole.

500g (1lb) young, tender carrots, scrubbed

2 tspn butter

2 tspn honey

**1** Place carrots in a saucepan and pour over enough cold water to just cover. Add butter and honey and bring to the boil.

**2** Lower heat, cover and simmer for 8-10 minutes, shaking pan occasionally, until carrots are tender and almost all the liquid evaporates. Serve immediately.

Serves 4

## Potatoes with Sun-dried Tomatoes

Store any remaining dressing in a covered jar in the refrigerator and serve with boiled pasta, salads, toasted Italian bread or steamed rice.

500g (1lb) new potatoes

**Sun-dried Tomato Dressing**

8-10 sun-dried tomatoes in oil, drained and roughly chopped

2 cloves garlic, crushed

185ml (6fl oz) olive oil

1 tblspn balsamic or red wine vinegar

chopped fresh herbs of your choice, optional

**1** To make dressing, place tomatoes and garlic in a blender or food processor and process until finely chopped. With machine running, slowly add oil and process until mixture thickens. Add vinegar and herbs (if using) and process to combine.

**2** Boil, steam or microwave potatoes until just tender. Drain and toss with 125ml (4fl oz) of the dressing. Serve warm.

Serves 4

## Fruit Fool

For an extra special touch serve this easy dessert with dessert biscuits or sponge fingers.

125g (4oz) dried apricots

315ml (10fl oz) boiling water

2 tblspn sugar

90-125ml (3-4fl oz) double cream, whipped

**Custard**

1 1/2 tblspn custard powder

1 tblspn sugar

250ml (8fl oz) milk

**1** Place apricots and boiling water in a small saucepan and set aside to cool. Add sugar and bring to the boil, stirring. Lower heat and simmer gently until apricots are tender. Set aside to cool, then purée.

**2** To make custard, combine custard powder and sugar in a saucepan and gradually stir in milk. Cook over moderate heat, stirring constantly, until mixture boils. Lower heat and simmer, stirring, for 2 minutes or until thick. Remove pan from heat and cover surface of custard with plastic food wrap. Cool.

**3** Fold custard into apricot purée, then fold in whipped cream to give a marbled effect. Spoon into dessert glasses or serving bowl and chill.

Serves 4-6

**Variations**
**Fresh Apricot Fool:** Stew 500g (1lb) stoned apricots with 250ml (8fl oz) water and sugar to taste. Purée and cool before using.
**Rhubarb Fool:** Cook 500g (1lb) trimmed and sliced rhubarb with 125g (4oz) sugar and 125ml (4fl oz) water over low heat until tender, purée and cool before using.
**Raspberry Fool:** Push 300g (9 1/2 oz) fresh raspberries through a sieve, discard seeds and use the purée.

*Carrots Vichy, Grilled Lamb Cutlets, Potatoes with Sun-dried Tomatoes*

## Braised Pork with Cider and Apples

Should you want crackling, ask the butcher to score the rind into strips for you. Before cooking the pork, bake rind in a preheated 425°C (220°F/ Gas 7) oven for 15-20 minutes or until puffed and crisp. Reheat just prior to serving.

*1.5kg (3lb) boned loin of pork, rind removed, rolled and tied*

*2 tspn salt*

*1 tspn choped fresh sage*

*1 tspn chopped fresh thyme*

*freshly ground black pepper*

*2 tblspn vegetable oil*

*2-3 onions, chopped*

*4 large cloves garlic*

*125ml (4fl oz) cider*

**Sautéed Apples**

*2 tblspn butter*

*1 large Granny Smith apple, cored and cut into 12 wedges*

*1 large red Delicious apple, cored and cut into 12 wedges*

**1** Pat pork dry with paper towels. Combine salt, herbs and black pepper to taste, rub over pork, then wrap in greaseproof paper and chill for 2-3 hours.

**2** Preheat oven to 180°C (350°F/ Gas 4). Heat oil in a flameproof casserole and cook pork over moderate heat until brown on all sides. Remove pork and discard all but 2 tablespoons fat. Add onions and garlic to casserole and sauté until golden. Return pork to casserole, add cider and bring to the boil. Cover and bake for 1-1¼ hours or until pork is cooked.

**3** To cook apples, melt butter in a large frying pan and cook apples over moderate heat, stirring, for 2-4 minutes or until golden.

**4** Transfer pork to a serving plate and keep warm. Skim excess fat from cooking juices. Purée juices and onions in a blender or food processor and serve with pork and apples.

*Serves 6-8*

## Carrot and Parsnip Purée

*1kg (2lb) carrots, chopped*

*1kg (2lb) parsnips, chopped*

*30g (1oz) butter*

*salt*

*freshly ground black pepper*

Boil, steam or microwave carrots and parsnips until tender. Drain and cool slightly. Place vegetables, in batches, in a blender or food processor and process to make a purée. Place purée in a saucepan, add butter and salt and black pepper to taste and stir over low heat until hot. Serve immediately.

*Serves 6-8*

## Peas, Celery and Spring Onions

*30g (1oz) unsalted butter*

*3 stalks celery, finely sliced*

*6-8 spring onions, finely sliced*

*375g (12oz) fresh shelled or frozen peas*

*60ml (2fl oz) water*

*1 tspn sugar*

*salt*

*freshly ground black pepper*

*few chopped celery leaves for garnish*

Melt butter in a heavy saucepan and cook celery and spring onions, covered, over low heat, shaking pan occasionally, for 5 minutes. Add peas, water and sugar and simmer, partially covered, until peas are tender — 15 minutes for fresh peas or 5 minutes for frozen peas. Season to taste and serve garnished with celery leaves.

*Serves 6-8*

## Bread and Butter Pudding

An old favourite becomes a dinner party special when made with Scottish highland flair.

*90g (3oz) sultanas*

*2 tblspn whisky*

*440ml (14fl oz) milk*

*60g (2oz) caster sugar*

*butter*

*8 thin slices white bread*

*4 tblspn orange marmalade*

*4 eggs*

*185ml (6fl oz) double cream*

*toasted flaked almonds*

*sifted icing sugar, for dusting*

**1** Soak sultanas in whisky for several hours. Scald milk with caster sugar in a saucepan over low heat, stirring until sugar dissolves. Cool.

**2** Butter bread generously and spread with half the marmalade. Make into sandwiches, trim off crusts and cut each diagonally into quarters. Arrange in a buttered 1 litre (1¾pt) ovenproof dish and sprinkle with undrained sultanas.

**3** Beat eggs and cream together, stir in milk mixture and pour over bread. Stand for 30 minutes.

**4** Preheat oven to 160°C (325°F/ Gas 3). Place dish in a roasting tin, pour in enough hot water to come halfway up the sides of the dish and bake for 50 minutes or until top is crisp and custard is set.

**5** Heat remaining marmalade with 1 teaspoon water and brush over pudding. Sprinkle with almonds and icing sugar.

*Peas, Celery and Spring Onions, Carrot and Parsnip Purée, Braised Pork with Cider and Apples*

# Index

Managing Editor: Rachel Blackmore
Editor: Linda Venturoni
Production Manager: Anna Maguire
Picture Editor: Kirsten Holmes
Production Editor: Sheridan Packer
Trainee Production Editor: Danielle Thiris
Editorial and Production Assistant: Katrina O'Brien
Cover Styling: Janet Mitchell

Published by J.B. Fairfax Press Pty Limited
80-82 McLachlan Avenue
Rushcutters Bay, NSW 2011
A.C.N. 003 738 430

Formatted by J.B.Fairfax Press Pty Limited
Printed by Toppan Printing Co, Hong Kong
PRINTED IN HONG KONG

© Margaret Fulton and Suzanne Gibbs (recipes)
© Ray Jarrett (photography)
© This edition J.B. Fairfax Press Pty Limited 1995
This book is copyright. No part may be reproduced or transmitted without the written permission of the publisher. Enquiries should be made in writing to the publisher.

JBFP 394 A/UK
Includes Index
ISBN 1 86343 116 0 (set)
ISBN 1 86343 227 2

Distribution and Sales Enquiries
**Australia:** J.B. Fairfax Press Pty Limited
Ph: (02) 361 6366 Fax: (02) 360 6262
**United Kingdom:** J.B. Fairfax Press Limited
Ph (01933) 402330 Fax: (01933) 402234